This book is for all those
who have a place in their
heart for a true love, but
who have yet to find him
or her.

Foreword

by John Assaraf
Contributor to The Secret and President of OneCoach.com

I met Sally in La Jolla at her art gallery in 2005 through a friend who wanted me to see the simplicity and elegance of her work. I was most impressed with how connected she was to her work and also how gentle she was with a confident certainty that she could accomplish whatever she chose.

Her colorful and expressive art resonated with every person who walked in the store. The energy was clean and fun and you felt great being in an environment that was full of life and love. That is Sally's energy.

Sally is always growing, evolving and most of all, giving of her spirit through her art and being. What you see is what you get with Sally. Simple, Honest, Certain and Loving.

In her latest work of art, "How to Get your Man", she shares her personal love story and lays out a very precise formula that any woman (or man) can apply to attract their perfect partner.

There is power in simplicity and what she shares in this mini "relationship" biography meets how to book, is her story of meeting the Prince Charming of her life and how you can follow your inner guidance and intelligence to find yours.

I have been studying and applying what is in this

book for over 25 years and I know from my own experiences and from finding my own very special partner that this process works like a miracle.

Each one of us has the ability to create and have our own love story. And Sally shows us how in this great little book.

Every second of ever day you and I are sending out energy signals that reach the farthest distances in the cosmos. Those signals are determined by our focus and personal energy field.

This book will show you exactly how to get perfectly clear on your perfect man (or woman) and make that dream your reality.

With all my love,
John

I don't know how I knew to do it, but I did. I knew how to get my man.

I hadn't always known. My long journey to the love of my life had many ups and downs, pitfalls and pratfalls, and I experienced many trials and errors before reaching the slam-dunk formula I will reveal to you here.

But first, my journey...

My love story begins as a girl of twenty-one. Before that, I focus on one single dream: to be a tennis champion. In my day, that means winning Wimbledon, and my entire waking life revolves around a tennis court. I go to school, of course, but before school and after school, it is all about tennis for me.

My athletic father is my co-conspirator in this dream. He works with me daily, finds me the best coach he can and hits millions of tennis balls to me. I hone my skills. With a tremendous amount of effort and determination I achieve a good deal of what we both set out to do.

Future tennis champion at 14.
Keeping an eye on the ball at 15.

U.S. Junior Champion at 18.

I win the U.S. and Wimbledon Junior Champion-ships, then become a Wimbledon semi-finalist in the Women's division. Since the age of ten, I have been climbing this ladder to success, determined to reach the top rung, to hit my target. Yes, next year surely is my year to win Wimbledon. Yet that next year, at the age of twenty-one, my heart turns my head in another direction. I find there is more to life than hitting tennis balls. I discover men! And that is the end of my Wimbledon quest.

My love life doesn't blossom without some build-up. There are boyfriends throughout my early years, darling boys dotting tennis courts from Burlingame to Santa Monica. As we practice our backhands and forehands we practice our flirting.

One exceptionally cute heartthrob by the name of Ricky Nelson steals my heart at the age of fifteen with his dancing feet and innocent kisses. Later he will steal many girls' hearts with his music.

Tender moments are not forgotten by the heart.

©2008 Sally Huss, Distributed by King Features Syndicate

In college at Occidental, my affairs of the heart grow a little stronger. There are fraternity boys and frat parties woven around studies and tennis practice. Some of my sorority sisters want only to finish school with an engagement ring on their finger. I see nothing interesting in that. For me, school is life's classroom, filled with intriguing males to learn from.

Then comes the magical year for me, when the boys turn into men!

The Music of Love

From my earliest years, I grow up on musicals, beautiful films mainly, with delightful soundtracks — "Annie Get Your Gun," "Showboat," "Guys and Dolls," "Oklahoma," "High Society," "The Music

Man," "My Fair Lady." The music is filled with romantic themes that plant the idea of idyllic love deep in my subconscious. I spend hours listening to these records as I skip rope and train, preparing for my next trip to England. Unbeknownst to them, Howard Keel, Gordon MacRae, Frank Sinatra and Robert Preston become my workout partners. I fall in love with them and the stories they tell in the songs they sing. One of my favorites is "Bye Bye Birdie," a silly farce of a musical, with songs ideal for rope skipping. By the time I am ready for Wimbledon and my push for the Championship, I know every word of every tune.

I begin the tournament season in Manchester, England competing in an event as a prelude to Wimbledon. The weather is dreary and I am still not used to the grass courts when I play an early round match. Even though I am highly seeded in the draw, I lose the match. It is my birthday, June 8, and I am all alone. My mood is as gray as the sky. I return to my room at the Midland Hotel and sit glum-faced in bed. Is this it? Is this going to be all there is to my birthday? No!

I leap to my feet. It is 9:45 p.m. and the dining room closes at 10. I grab a long black sweater dress, pull it on over my pajamas, throw a string of pearls around my neck, roll up my pajama legs, add some pumps and white gloves and run for the elevator.

A single pair of sweethearts lingers in the dining room, holding hands and sipping an aperitif by candlelight. I long for that kind of romance, but instead, I order a tasty feast and enjoy every bit of it.

Leaving the dining room I pass a private banquet hall where a song from my beloved "Bye Bye Birdie" fills the air. When a waitress emerges, I ask her what is going on. "Oh," she says, "the cast of 'Bye Bye Birdie' is celebrating one of the writers' birthday." I am beyond thrilled. I explain that it is my birthday too, and she disappears inside only to return with the star of the show. His name is Peter – the most attractive man I have ever seen. He explains that the cast is in Manchester preparing for their London opening. "Wouldn't you like to join us for some birthday cake?" he asks.

That piece of cake turns into dinners, and the dinners turn into breakfasts. I cannot imagine anything more exciting than falling in love...and falling in love in a musical.

This is it. Wimbledon is over for me. I go through the motions of competing in the tournament that year, but I only have eyes for the fun of sneaking

*Center Court
Wimbledon.*

backstage after a performance of "Birdie," dining with cast members in Soho and walking through London, holding hands with this most gorgeous man as he sings a love song to me right there on the street.

I may be young and inexperienced, but I know what feels good. And Peter feels very good.

I also know that he won't be mine forever. He has a wife and family in California. As much as I am in love with him, I know our romance is destined to end. I begin a new kind of training – that of being able to be in love, but not for keeps, no strings attached.

Along every path beautiful experiences are gathered.

©2006 Sally Huss, Distributed by King Features Syndicate

Peter and I go our separate ways a week later, after shedding a few tears, never expecting to see each other again. It is a sweet time with a very sweet man, and I still treasure those tender moments.

A Fine Romance

Once I am off of the tennis circuit it doesn't take me long to disengage myself from the habits and routines associated with being a champion. I am free now to enjoy my life in a different way. My happiness up to this point is predicated on winning tennis matches. Now I discover a whole new world of happiness to explore. Romance!

I return to California and enter the job market where I meet interesting men from all walks of life.

I work for a popular television personality in the Los Angeles area, Ralph Story, who sends me out on research assignments, but I do my own kind of research on the side. Everywhere I go – while collecting information on everything from five-star restaurants and private clubs to tattoo parlors and sports teams – I meet fascinating men. There are sportscasters and football stars, television executives and stockbrokers. They are fun to be with, dine with, dance with, but not to take home to mama. I'm not ready for anything serious.

A day without love is a day lost.

I enjoy a few years working at Goldwyn Studios for Samuel Goldwyn, Jr. There I can pop onto a sound stage and watch some of the most charming and dashingly handsome men at work, and some of them are fun to play with too.

On the set of The Young Lovers with Peter Fonda.

One day, David Jansen charges down a staircase while shooting a segment of The Fugitive. He grabs me where I stand. "Shall we dance?" he asks, his arms reaching for me. Why not? The idea of romance is a dance to me. And we dance our way around the set of his show for the next few months until my heart finds a new partner.

Affairs of the Heart

Sydney is a producer/director who is glamorous in every way. To me, he exudes old Hollywood charm and has everything I like in a man at that time – intelligence, sensitivity, good looks, great taste, status, a Jaguar...a wife and a house full of kids.

I meet Sydney when I am invited to play tennis on his court in Beverly Hills by a boyfriend of mine. No sooner do I set eyes on him, than I send the boyfriend away.

After playing tennis, Sydney and I lunch at the Beverly Hills Hotel. We park in his sports car on the side of the drive and he touches my hand as we talk, then he leans over and kisses me. My heart leaps. I can't help it, I am smitten. Everything about him is interesting to me – his work, his life, the texture of the clothes he wears, the smoothness of his skin. He smells good as only a well-groomed man of means can.

We talk of the future and I convince him that I have no interest in a long-term relationship, that I am only collecting wonderful memories that I can look back on one day when I am very old. It is a great line to free any man interested in me and it might even be something that I believe myself at the time.

This love affair sets in motion a whole chain of events that keeps me unsettled for quite some time. While it lasts, I no longer see myself in a musical as I do with Peter. I am now with the one who produces the musical. It is great.

There are romantic times in New York, going to

15

shows and fine restaurants. There are more romantic times at the beach, picnicking on the sand with wine and cheese, feeding grapes to one another. He is charming, attentive, dashing and elegant. He is also conveniently taken. I love every minute of it.

Each day is a lifetime to be lived fully, joyfully and without regret.

Eventually, like all things with no strings attached, we float apart.

A Free Spirited Woman

I take my next regular job as manager of Paul Simon's music publishing company. This is not without male incident either. I meet more fascinating men. Why wouldn't I? This is the time of brotherly love, universal consciousness, the Beatles and love-ins.

There is nothing I am particularly looking for with these relationships, other than to be in love. I want to feel it, inhale it, receive it and give it. I'm not looking for acceptance or reassurance. Marriage is not on my mind as it is on most young women's my age.

Who knows where this attitude comes from, but I'm not stopping to find out. I am having the time of my life with the life of my time as a young, vivacious, pretty woman. This boldness and self-confidence doesn't require a man to fulfill me, just love me.

Enjoying a game at the Racquet Club in Palm Springs.

I never think of the future or how I will live or how I will be in the times to come. It is all about what is happening now. I love my life just the way it is. I certainly am not willing to trust my heart completely to one man forever at this point. One day perhaps I will be interested in something permanent, but not now.

17

Joie de Vivre

In all this exploring and enjoying romantic adventures I secretly hold to one mantra: "you can never be too thin." I operate under the assumption that men like thin women. As a true competitor, if thin is the game, I will be the thinnest. With the use of a few pills here, a shot there, little caloric intake and near zero nourishment, I am definitely thin. Then I find you can be too thin.

Yes, too thin.

This lack of any substantial nourishment eventually leads to my physical collapse and sends me to a round of doctors, the wisest of which is Giovanni Boni, a homeopath and an acupuncturist. Dr. Boni very tactfully convinces me that I cannot live on nervous energy alone. I have to eat.

Beyond that, Dr. Boni has a secret elixir, his most

extraordinary wife, Therese. Besides being a master linguist, Therese is a master at life. The lessons she teaches in French contain life lessons as well. I sign up because I certainly need them.

The Bonis are people who know what life is about. They associate with the great spiritual masters in Europe and the U.S. The wisest of the wise, from Sufis to Swamis, flow through their home in West Los Angeles. I stay in the background and listen.

The pursuit of spiritual matters becomes my next great adventure. I am full of joy by this time, having gained a few pounds and a few insights. I have been exploring love on the physical level, now I venture into universal love through meditation.

Love is all there is worth having or giving or being.

©2006 Sally Huss, Distributed by King Features Syndicate

I mediate each morning. A theme surfaces. Then a little vision-story plays itself out in my head. I get up, write it down, illustrate it and bind it, never knowing what these stories will be used for.

Dr. Boni eventually sends me to a colleague of his, Dr. Martha Frank, a renowned psychologist. She asks me to bring some of my artwork and stories for our visit. I share them with her. I dance for her and we talk. And she says, "You have such joie de vivre, where is the man in your life?"

During this recuperative period and exploration of spiritual matters, I totally leave the playing field of romance behind. Yes, where is the man? I once have plenty of boyfriends, even a couple of engagements, but no one I am truly serious about. No one whom I want to marry or is available to marry. Perhaps this is the time. I feel settled and balanced, purified and more able to handle responsibilities. I turn a corner. Am I growing up? Yes, a man could be just the thing. But not any man – My Man.

My Letter to the Sun

So I set about to create my man. Again, I'm not sure how I know to do it, but I do. After much thought, I have a plan and I know it will work.

I write a letter to the Sun. I know the Sun is a very powerful and knowing being. After all, we live by his grace, his warmth and light. From my spiritual experiences I am aware that everything is alive, everything is conscious. It is a matter of degree. Therefore, I want to seek help from the most powerful and miraculous being I see in the physical realm. The Sun is perfect.

Here is what I write:

"Dear Sun, please send me My Man." I am tired of

other people's men. They are fun and romantic for a time, but now I am looking for a "keeper."

Then I write, "Here are the qualities of My Man:"

• He is Loving. To me, being a loving person is the most important thing on my list. I feel love is the most important thing in life. So I want him to be loving. I want him to make me feel loved and appreciated. I want him to honor and respect our love and that, at all times, it is given the highest priority in our lives, and continues through all circumstances – good ones and difficult ones. This is a love that sustains us in all situations. This is what I want in My Man.

Of all that matters, love matters most.

• He is Kind. Just like loving, kindness is necessary. A kind man who appreciates others and cares about their situations, their struggles, is important to me. I want a warm-hearted man, not just for me, but someone who benefits others by his mere presence – a man who contains kindness.

21

Kindness is good.
Kindness is wise.
Kindness is necessary.

©2006 Sally Huss, Distributed by King Features Syndicate

• He is Good. I want a really good man, good to the core, a person whose intentions are always the best. My experience around high-powered men leads me to realize that their intentions are not always good. For me, good is a spiritual quality of true greatness. My Man is without trickiness and deviousness. He is trustworthy. He chooses ways and directions for us that are always good, never sacrificing his integrity. He wants the best for me, for us and for others around us.

(Am I asking too much? As long as I am creating him I might as well make him the best I can.)

Goodness matters,
for goodness sake!

©2007 Sally Huss, Distributed by King Features Syndicate

• He is Intelligent. Oh yes, I want an intelligent man, one who is smarter than me. He is someone who is clear-thinking and has a curious mind, someone who is not stuck mentally, but is open-minded and welcomes new ideas. He loves learning and values intellectual challenges. He is someone to help me figure out the best direction when a fork in the road appears. Up to this point my pattern is to take the path of the heart exclusively and sometimes that is not the most intelligent way to proceed. So, a smart man who is old enough to have gathered a good bit of wisdom is what I want.

Life includes you in its every thought.

• He is Generous. My Man is someone who easily shares himself and what he has, and is delighted to do so. I want him to tip generously and drop bills in the Salvation Army's buckets at Christmastime. I want him to buy me things spontaneously, not necessarily expensive things, but meaningful, memorable things – a funny hat, a picture frame with his picture in it, a vase for flowers. Things I can treasure.

Big-hearted people show themselves for what they are by what they do.

Generosity, to me, is a sub-category of goodness. A self-confident man who is generous with himself and his things knows that there is a never-ending abundance from which he can give. (I once know a man who took the same can of tennis balls from court to court for over a year, never opening it. He's the kind who doesn't know about giving. He doesn't know about supply.)

• He is Happy. Equal on my list to loving is being happy. I want a happy, optimistic man, one who knows his own worth and relishes it, one who greets me with a smile, one who loves life. He needs to be happy because my plan is we are doing happy things together. We travel. We discover new restaurants, hold hands in the movies, climb mountains, fish in remote lakes and swim in turquoise blue seas. I want to go to all the places that I know and love with him and I want him to take me to his special places as well. He loves music and even dances, but he doesn't have to be crazy about it. (I have never met a really terrific man who is a terrific dancer.) But, he definitely has to be happy.

Happy days are made by happy people.
Happy people are made by choice.

©2008 Sally Huss, Distributed by King Features Syndicate

● He is Athletic. It is wonderful if he is athletic, even better if he plays tennis. I know our life together will take us to unusual, exciting places, beautiful places – mountains, oceans and deserts. But those places are better if we enjoy each other in activities we love – like tennis.

Celebrity event with Ricardo Montalban, Rick Berry, MacDonald Carey.

25

So I put this request down on my list. There are fabulous places to go and interesting people to meet all connected to tennis. (I am invited to several pro-celebrity tennis events each year from Pebble Beach to Palm Beach and it will be more fun if My Man is included.)

• He Wants a Family. He loves children and appreciates family life. I might wish to have a child one day and I want My Man to want this too. I come from a traditional family where children and family are valued above all else. I want someone who thinks the same.

• He is Responsible. Responsibility is also a sub-category of good in my book. A responsible man is what my father is and his father before him. They are good people who take charge and take care of their own. They are honorable men. My tendency in the past is to be a bit flighty, but in my center I am a very responsible person and want the same of My Man.

• He is Handsome. Why not? No one else has to think he is handsome, but I want a man who is handsome to me. This does not mean a man with movie-star looks, but a sturdy, healthy, solid, wholesome, good-looking man. That is perfect.

• He is Faithful. In my heart of hearts I am monogamous and again I want the same of My Man. I understand the wandering hearts of some men. Yet romance will remain in my marriage, I am sure of it.

Yes, it is marriage that I am asking for now. A real

down to earth, full-fledged , stick together through thick or thin, for better or worse – marriage!

These are the qualities of my man I ask for in my letter to the Sun. I do leave room at the bottom of the page to add more qualities later if I think of some, but this does it for now.

Then I thank the Sun, sign my name and tape my letter to a window where the Sun can see it, but where no one else can. I know by this time that thoughts are things and I do not want anyone putting their thoughts on my things, like my letter.

Believing in My Dream

Next, I get ready. I make sure my little apartment is clean, orderly and harmonious. It is already filled with light, but I need to add a few things, like a proper tea set. I'm sure my man will like to sit and sip a cup of tea with me while we enjoy each other's company.

It only takes one true love to fill a room.

And a rocking chair! It isn't that he is old, but rather that he enjoys the pleasant feeling of the movement while taking in the peacefulness of my space. A white wicker rocker is called for. Music. I line up my most romantic albums, then add a few. My man loves music, especially love songs. A new set of sheets are in order. I do whatever I think adds to the comfort of my man to make him feel at home.

I look in the mirror and size myself up. I am a little skinny by anyone's account. A few pounds need to be added, so I prepare to bulk up. Because I am teaching tennis and playing social tennis, I remain trim, but trim with some curves is better. I eat a little more.

Next, I get an appointment with Hollywood's most popular hairdresser at the time, Peter York, who styles my hair into a lovely, soft pageboy. A little trim for $200 seems appropriate for such an auspicious occasion, the meeting with my man.

A perfect trim.

In her day my mother is a traditional woman, a wonderful mother and homemaker. She sees me careen off of several walls in my life, not necessarily understanding my actions, but always loving me regardless. She kindly leaves me a little money in her will. She would love my new direction and in her absence she supports it. The money she leaves me is just enough to put the finishing touches on a future bride.

Shopping is in order. I need to go shopping. I stop into my favorite haunt, Country Club Fashions in Beverly Hills. When I walk in the saleslady asks me what I am looking for. "A dress," I say. She wants to know for what occasion. "My wedding," I answer.

She helps me pick out a beautiful teal green silk crepe number. It goes perfectly with some shoes I already have.

Once I have the surface details in place, the most important part of my formula is the work I do internally, inside my mind and heart.

Selfishly guard the heart's ability to love, then generously share its contents.

I make it a ritual. Every night I look at my Sun Letter on the window and think about my man and our life together. I imagine how our life will be – the things we do together, where we live and the places we visit. I imagine too that we are married. Then I send him love from my heart. I pretend he is away on a trip and coming home to me. I am in love with him before I ever meet him. That is the secret – I am in love before I ever have someone to be in love with. I go about my daily activities, beaming as only a woman in love can.

Next, I pay attention to my inner voice when it tells me to go somewhere or do something. I accept all invitations to gatherings and events. I don't know where or when he may show up. I just know he will. I continue to meditate early in the mornings, but only for a short time. And I still create my little stories.

Learning to love listening to the heart is a skill of infinite value.

©2008 Sally Huss, Distributed by King Features Syndicate

Courting My Love

I play social tennis and also teach my special Zen tennis on private courts in Beverly Hills and Malibu.

Creative people seem to like my way of playing and I always have interesting students – Helen Reddy, Milos Forman, Barbra Streisand, Marilyn Bergman, Jill St. John, Joel Grey, Larry Hagman and Kirk Douglas are a few.

Social tennis with George Stevens, Jr., Robert and Ethel Kennedy.

The court I teach on in Beverly Hills belongs to Jennings Lang who is head of television film production at Universal Studios. Jennings is a kind and generous man who encourages me in my artwork and also refers actors and other VIPs to me for tennis lessons. It is on his court that I meet Vasili, the first man who proposes marriage to me that year.

Vasili is a good friend of Milos Forman and a

Czechoslovakian artist who paints political themes. He is brought to Jennings' home by Milos to show his work. Jennings is a great collector of art and a soft touch to help a visiting artist such as Vasili. Vasili is an impressive man, dark, strong, romantic with penetrating eyes that he directs at me.

As the four of us sit together in the tennis house near the pool, with Brancusis and Henry Moores enhancing the garden, Vasili's art lay heavy and somber on the table, but his attention rests on me. And while Milos promotes his friend's art to Jennings, the friend promotes himself to me.

We go for lunch. We go for tea. We go for dinner. He vows his love and is sure I am the one for him. As many good qualities as he has, I am not sure that until-death-do-us-part is the right scenario with this man. I go back to my apartment, look at my Sun Letter and try to match the man with my list of requirements. They don't match.

The more you love, the more you will love.

As much as he thinks I am the one for him, he definitely is not the one for me. As good a person as he is he lacks the lightness and joy that I expect in my man. Even though my heart goes pitter pat, it does not go pitter pat for him. No, Vasili is not my man.

Following my plan to accept all invitations, I am invited to play tennis in an international tournament in a small town outside of Lagos, Nigeria. All expenses are paid, so I pack up my bags, rackets and heart and off I go.

Man number two shows up on a dance floor in Nigeria.

It happens like this. Because the heat is so unbearable in this venue, all the players in the tournament practice in the mornings, rest during the day before playing their matches in the evenings. After that, the players dance all night. At least I do.

Love beckons to all of us, whether we know it or not.

It is under the twinkling lights on a patio dance floor that I meet Richard, suitor number two. He is a successful English entrepreneur who has a lucrative lumber business in the area. He is charming, entertaining, thoughtful, intelligent, handsome, rich – and a good dancer. I like his European flair, his ruddy good looks and the way he makes me feel: like a princess he adores. He is quite sure I am the one for him and falls in love with me almost upon meeting.

It is what I am sending out, I later realize, that draws these men to me. But as attractive as Richard is, and as many fine qualities as he possesses, I never imagine in all my imaginings that I will be living with my man in a place so remote and unbearably hot as Nigeria. In his kindness he nurses me through a bad case of malaria, sees me safely on my plane back to the U.S. and accepts my rejection of his proposal of marriage with graciousness.

The Look of Love

I return to California and continue my happy plan – meditating, creating books, playing and teaching tennis and dreaming of my Sun Man. In the books I write and illustrate, several interesting characters begin to appear – a beautiful woman with lovely soft under-turned hair, a handsome man and a little boy. In one story the little boy has a pet rabbit.

Besides teaching on Jennings' court, I am occasionally invited to play social tennis there on weekends with a group of his friends. And again true to my vow of saying "yes" to all invitations, I agree to play in a group one Saturday morning in October. Jennings' secretary adds one suggestion, "Bring some of your artwork. A man from Hallmark is going to be there!"

Jennings Lang hard at play.

Of course. Of course. Jennings is always trying to help my artistic career and even thinks I could do a feature for newspapers combining my thoughts with my illustrations. Little does he know that many years later, this idea comes to fruition. But at this point he thinks Hallmark might be perfect for me.

So on the day I am to meet the man from Hallmark I put on my prettiest tennis dress, dab on my favorite perfume, Fracas, gather up my artwork and tennis racket and head for Jennings' home. As I walk through the sculpture garden, meandering down toward the court there is the sweet smell of something special in the air.

This court is my favorite of all the courts I have

ever played on. Situated in a ravine, surrounded by eucalyptus trees, it needs no tarps. The trees provide the backdrop and the birds provide the music.

I sit by the side of the court, waiting my turn to play while the other players finish their set.

I am called onto the court to be Jennings' partner. Across the net is Alan Bergman, the songwriter, and Marv Huss, the man from Hallmark. As Marv reaches for my hand in greeting, his smile overwhelms me with warmth. He is delicious, an oatmeal cookie, an all-American type, wholesome and handsome at the same time, and a bit old-fashioned like his name. There is a force about him that makes me know I should pay attention to this man, and not just for my artwork.

Marv Huss ready to play.

I have a hard time focusing on the ball as we play. I pass him a few times at the net. He laughs. He puts away my lobs. I laugh. He is someone I know, but am just meeting for the first time.

We sit courtside after the tennis and he rummages through my portfolio, making complimentary and encouraging remarks. Once we are done with that, I don't want our time together to end, so I ask if he has played enough tennis for the day.

"No," he says.

"Well, I'm going out to Malibu to play some more," I say. "Would you like to go along?"

And he says, "Yes."

We motor out to the Malibu Colony in my MG. It is where I teach tennis when I'm not on Jennings' court. There on the Colony's drive, across from the houses on the ocean side, are matching tennis courts, nearly one for every other house. I am given keys to many of them, treasured items for non-court owners. The local hardware store does a brisk business in keys with players who do not have a court, but who have gotten their hands on a key.

Everyone wins in tennis because everyone starts with love!

On this day Marv and I meander down the lane until we come upon some of my tennis buddies, Bob MacLeod, in his 60's and still editor of Teen Magazine, Albie Linnick, a rogue attorney, Dick Greenberg, a real estate mogul and Jack Warden, the actor. We are welcomed in and play a round or two, then slip through Bob's house to the beach.

It is here, I think, that I fall in love with this man from Hallmark. As we walk along, he tells me of his life, his work as head of advertising for Hallmark, his admiration for its founder, Joyce Hall, whom he works for directly, and his efforts in providing the best possible programs for the Hallmark Hall of Fame. That's why he is in town, to purchase the rights to "The Snow Goose" from Universal Studios for the television series.

In all this small talk, he reveals himself. I know the core of this man is good. His intentions, his gestures and his words are kind and generous. He matches my enthusiasm for life. He is heartfelt and I am heart struck. Our conversation continues over dinner and dancing. It is a perfect day.

Love changes everything!

©2008 Sally Huss, Distributed by King Features Syndicate

Before I put my head on my pillow that night I take my Sun Letter off the window and read it again. He is everything on my list — Marv is the one. There is no question about it from my point of view. He is my dream come true. He is my Sun Man.

It takes two more years before we finally get together. There are a few obstacles to be cleared out of the way. He lives across the country from me and has a very exciting career with responsibilities that have to be attended to. So during that time Marv sends me cards from Hallmark and I send him card designs for Hallmark. I send him a pair of sunglasses which he says he is forever losing. He sends me cards from Hallmark. Our favorite song by Stevie Wonder includes the words, "You are the sunshine of my life. You're the apple of my eye." So I send him a crystal apple to put on his desk. He sends me cards from Hallmark. Then he leaves Hallmark and moves from Kansas City to Denver to start his own advertising agency.

Sweeter than candy
are the words
from a loved one.

To pass the time waiting for Marv's life to rearrange itself, I go back on the Virginia Slims Tennis Circuit. When the tour passes through Denver, Marv and I meet again. Sitting in the stands on center court after one of my matches, we map out our future together. His career is changed, but he is ready to change once more.

He has enough of corporate life and wearing ties. We decide to teach tennis together and perhaps run a club together, if we can find one.

When I finish the tour I move to Colorado Springs to be closer to him and he in turn restructures his living situation to be with me.

A perfect match.

Happy in love.

During my time in Colorado Springs I make contact with a man who wants to build a resort in Aspen. He needs a manager to oversee the construction and manage the project. And he needs a head rackets pro. Both of us fill the bill.

Life and Love with My Man

Marv and I are married on a beautiful fall morning in Aspen in 1976. We spend three glorious years there building The Aspen Club and filling it with members. During that time we welcome our wonderful son Michael into the world. Five years later our son is given a rabbit for Easter, just as I envision in one of my little books.

Wedding in Aspen.

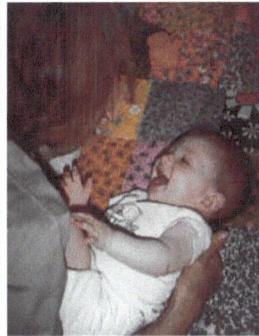

And baby makes three.

Our life together is full of extraordinary experiences and enriched by outstanding people we meet along the way. All of this life with Marv is foretold in pictures and words, called forth through the Law of Attraction by my Sun Letter, my imagination and my love for what I want.

It is over 35 years since creating my Sun Letter and my Sun Man lives up to my expectations and more. It doesn't mean that we live happily-ever-after without some bumps in the road, some unexpected turn of events. Yet during these learning curves and growing cycles, we remain devoted to each other and supportive of one another.

Fun with son.

Still celebrating.

At various times we operate a resort in the mountains of Colorado, develop a sports clothing line in North Carolina, and sell real estate in the deserts and beaches of California. Now we work together spreading my art and writing. Marv's abilities as a marketer and businessman are the perfect compliment to my artistic talents and through this we are able to create a business that benefits many. Our love for

42

each other is deep and sustains us both.

I remain forever grateful to Hallmark for caring enough to send the very best.

A gallery full of products.

Happy at work.

How To Get Your Man

The simple formula I used to get my man can help you find yours. It is simple. Anyone can do it. Finding your true love may seem like trying to find a needle in a haystack. But it is easy for the Sun. Just ask. Here is my formula:

1. Decide exactly what you want. Is it a life companion or just a friend? Is it a marriage or just a relationship? Be clear on this. You will get what you want. You need to make sure you want what you get.

2. Write a letter to the Sun describing the person you want to bring into your life. If you are looking for him, he is looking for you. But, describe this person in detail. Make sure you put down the most important character traits and qualities that you want in your person. Is honesty a quality you want? How about compassionate and considerate? Is a sense of humor important to you? Does he like kids? Is he athletic? Does he like opera, footballs games, or both? Does it matter if he is "successful?"

3. Put the letter where the Sun can see it, if possible, but it is not absolutely necessary. You can even put it in a drawer, if you like. But put it where no one else will see it.

4. Think about your life together, you and your man, the things you'll do, the places you'll go, where

you'll live. Think about the quality of your life and how your life will benefit others by the two of you being together.

5. Get ready. Put your house in order. That means clean up, straighten up. Look in the mirror and fix things. Who you attract will be your mirror. Make yourself attractive and worthy in every way of the person you are asking for. I've talked to women who say they would like to bring a man into their life, but they make no effort to pull themselves together. They remain messy and sometimes out of shape, hoping that a man will discover their inner beauty. Their thinking is that they will get their act together when he shows up. Too late! Get ready first.

6. Follow your inklings, your intuition, your inner knowing. Go places, meet people, be spontaneous. If you feel like taking a trip somewhere, do it. If you feel like trying a new restaurant, do it. He can't find you if you sit at home alone.

7. Be in love now! Don't wait until your man arrives. Enjoy the benefits of being in love right now. No one else has to know what you are up to, but you must be up to love. It is an irresistible force. It is the force that will bring him to you. He is no further than your thought of him and that thought will warm your heart.

*Way beyond words
is the heart.
Fortunately, it's
so close.*

©2007 Sally Huss, Distributed by King Features Syndicate

This is my formula. It has worked for me and it will work for you. Naturally it will work for anything you want to bring into your life whether it's finding a job, a place to live, or developing a creative passion. But bringing the love of your life into your life is the ultimate as far as I'm concerned. Focusing on what you want, engaging your heart and taking action cannot help but bring great results.

Success Stories

Over the years I have passed on this formula to others and they have passed it on to others too. I haven't kept track of the many successes, as there have been many. Here are just a few:

WILLIAM

One of the first people I ever shared the Sun Letter formula with was William. He was an older fellow who only wanted a girlfriend, someone to share dinner and a movie with. He created his Sun Letter, put it in the window on the third floor of his high-rise building and very soon she arrived. And, simply she wanted nothing more than the same – a boyfriend to go to dinner with and see a movie.

JOAN and BILL

Joan worked for Marv on a real estate project in Laguna Beach. She was small, clean-cut and cute-as-a-button, a former cheerleader at USC. Unfortunately, she had been married twice to men who were abusive.

As Joan and I sat together at a Christmas dinner party, she told me her story and her desire to be married to a wonderful man. I told her about the Sun Letter. As we spoke another woman at the table overheard our conversation and piped up.

Gail was a high-powered real estate agent, who handled sales of high-end condos in the Long Beach area. She had been married several times, but explained how she had finally brought into her life the perfect husband. She too wrote a letter. In her case, it was a very small note that she wore on her person. She placed the note inside her bra. It described the man she wanted and eventually got, even though she had very specific needs as far as living arrangements were concerned. She had to live part of the time in Long Beach and part in Los Angeles. All of this was taken into account. There was another unusual request she had, which was for a man who was "financially astute," not rich. Asking for a rich man had a flaw in the formula for Gail, and she had the track record to prove it.

Rich is a matter of the heart.

©2006 Sally Huss, Distributed by King Features Syndicate

Buoyed by Gail's success, Joan left the party determined to write her Sun Letter.

Meanwhile, I was teaching a little tennis in the Fallbrook area and overseeing our son Michael while Marv worked on the project in Laguna Beach. A friend of mine came forward and said, "You must work with Bill. He lost his wife of forty years to cancer and he is just miserable. He is depressed and lonely. Give him some lessons."

My lessons tended to end up being more than just tennis. And so it was with Bill. After a couple of lessons on the court, Bill opened up and began telling me how empty his life was. He had gone out on a few dates, but none of this mattered to him. He had been truly in love with his wife and now he didn't know what to do.

I asked, "Have you ever thought about being in love again?"

He looked startled, "No!"

"Well, would you like to?" He said he would. That was the opening I needed, so I told him about the Sun Letter.

He got so excited. "I know this is going to work! I know it!"

At our next tennis session he asked if he could add some pictures to the letter. "Of course," I said. "Cut pictures out from magazines, draw them, whatever. Yes. Yes."

The next thing I knew was that he had made a whole vision board about his dream woman and their life together. Then I got to thinking. Bill is small, clean-cut, cute-as-a-button and liked to dance. Then I remembered Joan liked to dance. When I told him about her, he insisted that I get her down for a visit. That weekend Joan joined Marv, Bill and me for dinner and dancing.

Dancing with the feet is one thing. Dancing with the heart is another.

©2008 Sally Huss, Distributed by King Features Syndicate

They were married six weeks later and are still married today, twenty-three years later. He put her on a pedestal where she belonged and he never took her down.

DOROTHY

Dororthy worked for us. She ran one of our galleries and did a fine job of it. Dorothy is a grand woman in all ways. She is big – well over six feet and an imposing figure. She has a presence that warrants her stature – solid, intelligent, intuitive, reliable and creative, and yet there was not a man in her life. Once upon a time, one stayed long enough to give her two fine children. But when she came to work for us there was no man, only a longing for one.

Now if you saw Dorothy you might think that it would be almost impossible to find an appropriate man for her outside of the NBA. But Dorothy trusted my counsel and prepared her Sun Letter. Now she is happy at heart with a terrific man in her life. She flies to San Francisco for a visit every week or so, and he flies to San Diego. I'm sure when her children have left the nest for good, Dorothy will fly to San Francisco and never return.

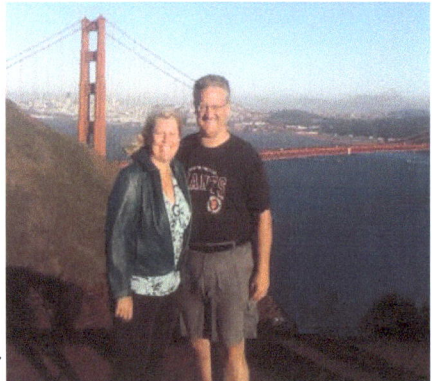

Dorothy with her Sun Man.

RUSTY

At one of the senior tennis tournaments in Newport Beach where I was playing, I passed on the formula to one of the players, Rusty. Months later at another tournament, she called me over to show me a picture of her daughter and her daughter's Sun Man. He was flying down from San Francisco that weekend to meet his future mother-in-law. The mother had passed the formula on and she couldn't have been happier.

Heart-touches move us beyond ourselves.

©2007 Sally Huss, Distributed by King Features Syndicate

MARY

During the National 40's tournament at the La Jolla Beach and Tennis Club in California one year, my friend from the Virginia Slims Tour days was bemoaning the fact that she had not come up with "her" man. Marv, who was very fond of Mary, said to me, "Tell her about the Sun Letter!" So I did.

Not long after that Mary called to tell us to watch

the Buffalo Bills' game on Monday Night Football. We did and when the camera panned to the owner's box there was Mary sitting so elegantly next to Ralph Wilson, owner of the Bills.

Now eighteen years later, as Mrs. Wilson, Mary still accompanies Ralph to the games, but also supports numerous good causes with Ralph's money.

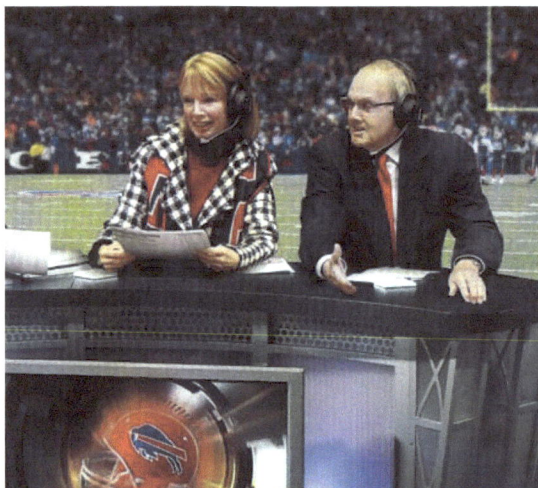

Mary and Ralph promoting the Bills.

I have given the Sun Letter formula to many people over the years. When I've run into some of them, I have asked about the results. There are, of course, the success stories, but it is interesting that some have not put the formula into practice, even though they know it will work. This leads me to believe that there is a right time for its use and it should not be used before that time, before someone really means it.

A Happy Ending

As I've suggested earlier, this same formula can

be applied to other things such as finding a job, a career, a school, an apartment, a home or even to creating a desired lifestyle. It is the setting in motion of an intention which, through the infallible Law of Attraction, brings to you what you want, what your heart is truly set on.

Dream big, plan well, work hard, smile always and good things will happen.

Long ago Jennings Lang suggested to me that I do a feature for newspapers with my thoughts and art. Now forty years later my panel called *Happy Musings* is syndicated by King Features and runs in newspapers across the country and on various internet sites. It was a long journey for that intention to come into being. But it happened.

One of those Musings states: Picture a happy life and soon you will be able to put a frame around it." That's what I did and you can too.

John Assaraf, one of the experts featured in The Secret and president of OneCoach.com, recently invited visitors to his website to participate in his new book included in The Complete Vision Board Kit. He asked for vision board stories – those real life happenings that had come true by putting images down on a board or paper. I saw the request on the very day the offer to participate was to expire. With only a half hour left before the deadline ended, I wrote how I had created a life in a notebook by drawing and writing stories about a family (a husband, wife, a little boy and a rabbit) that eventually became my life. The story was accepted and is the first chapter in his book.

I went to a special event launching The Complete Vision Board Kit and was given a signed copy by John. Later that night I read how John had brought his beautiful wife Maria into his life. Shortly after they met, he showed her his written description of his dream woman. As John says, "She was stunned. Here on paper, in black and white, was a thorough, detailed description of her. It wasn't someone like her – it was her…it couldn't have possibly been anyone but her."

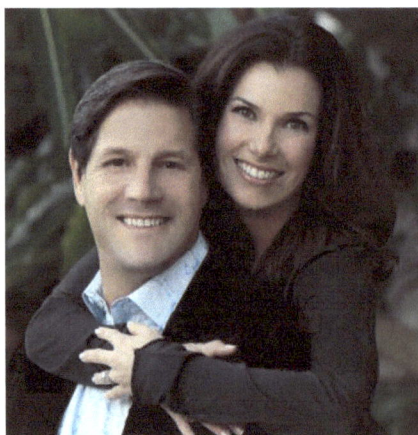

John and Maria.

When a request is made to the Sun, God, the Universe, Source, Infinite Intelligence, or your Higher Self it is an appeal made to that which is all-knowing, all-powerful of which you are a part. When that request is true and the intention set, the heart puts wings on it and the request returns fulfilled.

In these times of great change when there are few things you can count on to remain steady and stable, many people are looking for love and the warmth it brings. Who can blame them? The heart longs to belong to someone. If you are looking for your someone, this slam-dunk formula will help you find him or her. It worked for me. It has worked for others. It will work for you.

For every heart
there is a sweetheart.

©2007 Sally Huss, Distributed by King Features Syndicate

Valentine's Day is a special day reserved for sweethearts. May Valentine's Day be your special day in the future. It has been mine for over thirty-five years for nothing more than writing a letter to the Sun.

This is my love story. Now go create yours!

A Request

When you do create your love story, send it to lovestory@sallyhuss.com or P.O. Box 206, La Jolla, CA 92038.

Sally would love to read it. She is collecting these stories for her next book to inspire others and help keep romance alive.

An Invitation

You may go to www.sallyhuss.com to preview or purchase Sally's other books, including 10 Great Thoughts on Love and 10 Great Thoughts on Friendship, and also recieve her latest *Happy Musings* free.

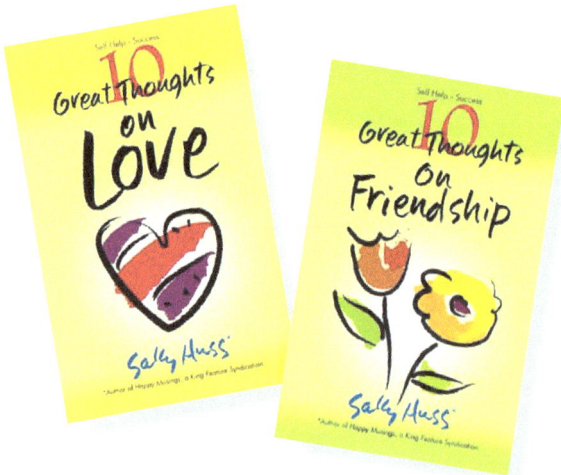